YOU ARE MY WORLD

YOU ARE MY WORLD

How a Parent's Love Shapes a Baby's Mind

AMY HATKOFF

STEWART, TABORI & CHANG | NEW YORK

For parents everywhere, whose love has the power to change the world.

And for Grandma Doe, who changed mine.

With all my love to Juliana, Isabella, Lilly, Nina, Jack, Chloe, Riley, Danielle, and Alyson, who bring light to us every day.

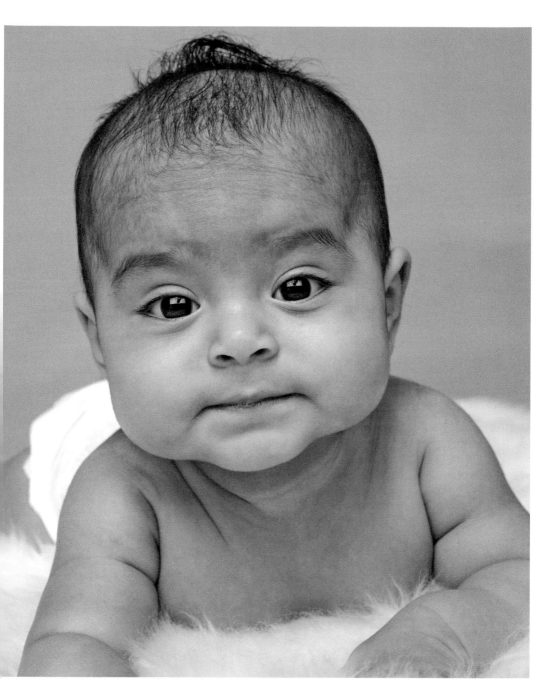

YOU ARE MY WORLD celebrates the impact a parent's love and attention has on a baby's development. It portrays the significant role that small, everyday moments have in shaping a baby's sense of self and capacity to learn. Science tells us that the brain develops through the dance that occurs between parents and children. In this book, babies do the talking and ask parents to join them in the dance.

We know that children's minds are shaped by experience. The way we touch, hold, talk to, look at, and respond to a baby affects that baby's self-image, view of the world, and his or her role in it. We are sending messages to our babies all the time. It is the seemingly insignificant exchanges with the significant people in their lives that teach a child who he or she is and can become.

In the infinite wisdom of nature, the simple exchanges that occur in the give and take of the parent-child relationship do the very complex work of wiring the neural pathways in the baby's brain. There is now scientific evidence that the loving act of gazing into your baby's eyes, for example, helps to develop self-awareness and sensitivity to others. The warmth of your skin, the gentleness of your touch, the tone of your voice, the softness of your smile are all building blocks for your baby's healthy development. The minutes, hours and days spent loving your baby, making a fool of yourself talking in high-pitched voices, dancing together to your favorite tunes, or just sitting with your infant and cooing are worth their weight in gold. You are building the solid foundation for your baby's future.

The small dance steps of everyday experience create secure attachments, known to be essential for all aspects of healthy development. Yet, in our fast-paced world with its emphasis on success, independence, and achievement, babies are often pushed to be on their own before they are ready. Parents can be made to feel that the kind of responsiveness and attunement that builds secure attachments will spoil the baby and make the child too needy or dependent. The research tells us that the opposite is true—that we foster independence by meeting a baby's needs consistently and promptly. *You Are My World* explores the value of responding to your baby from your own heart and in your own rhythm.

The text, while often poetic, is based on the latest scientific research on infant brain development. For example, "Your love melts my fear," addresses the fact that loving interactions between parents and babies release oxytocin, the "love hormone." Oxytocin increases trust and new research demonstrates that sufficient production of this hormone in infancy is essential to the capacity to love throughout life. Simple gestures, lifelong benefits.

The words herein are written with profound respect for the power of a parent's love. They are meant to illuminate a baby's sheer delight in, desire for, and receptivity to that love. The unfolding and development of a baby is nothing short of a miracle. *You Are My World* celebrates the role of a parent's love in that miracle and captures the extraordinary impact of the "ordinary" acts of parenting.

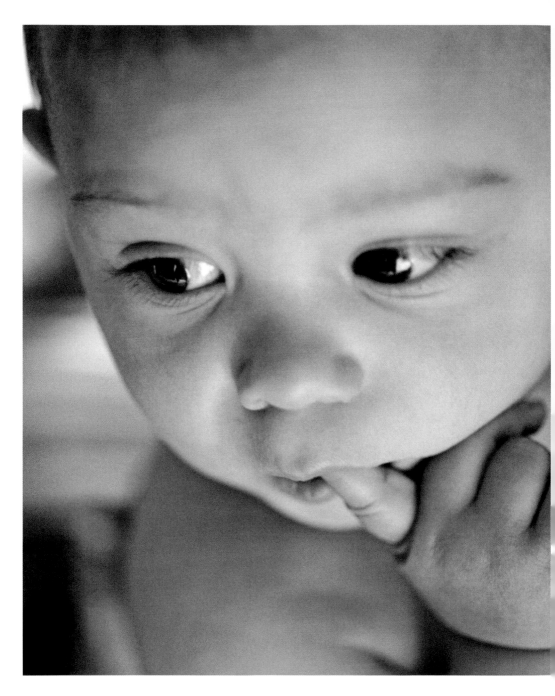

I KNOW YOU RIGHT FROM THE START.
I COULD PICK YOU OUT IN A CROWD.

I AM BORN READY
TO CONNECT.

IT'S HOW I'M WIRED.

**YOUR LOVE IS MY
FIRST TEACHER.**

**WHEN I CAN COUNT ON YOU,
I LEARN TO TRUST.**

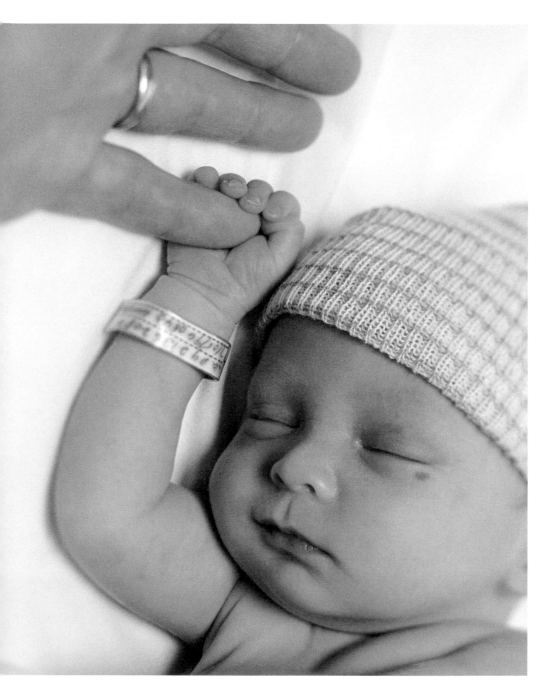

THE FIRST MILESTONE

Learning to trust is the main developmental task of the first year of life. When a baby learns to trust during this period, his or her brain will be wired to trust throughout life. Trust develops when a baby can count on his or her needs being met, knows that a parent is emotionally available, and has soothing routines. Responsive, sensitive parenting gives a baby's brain the message that the world is a safe place and that people are dependable.

**WHEN YOU UNDERSTAND ME,
YOU HELP ME TO
UNDERSTAND THE WORLD.**

YOU ARE MY MIRROR.

WHEN YOU SMILE AT ME, I LEARN THAT I AM LOVABLE.

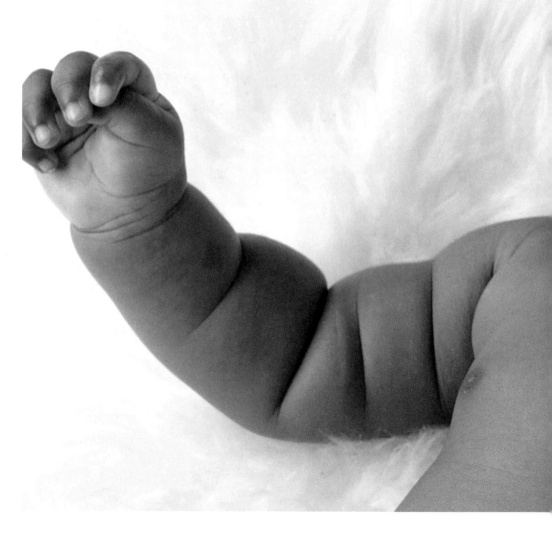

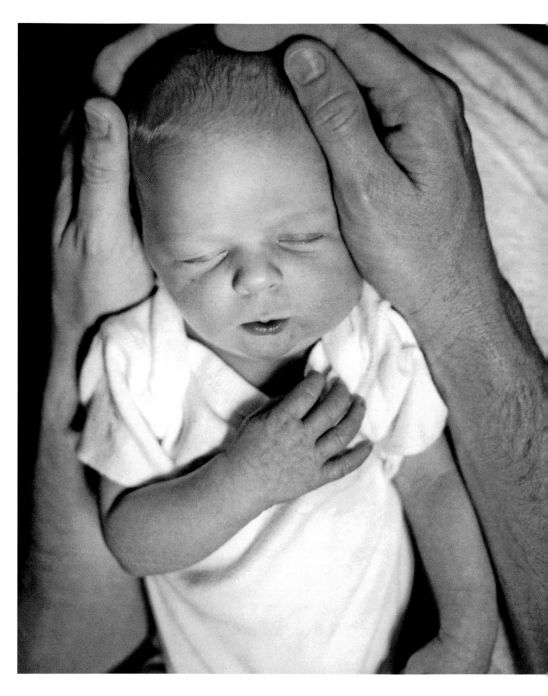

YOUR TOUCH IS LIKE MAGIC.

IT HELPS ME DEVELOP IN EVERY WAY.

WHEN YOU HOLD ME, I FEEL SAFE AND SECURE.

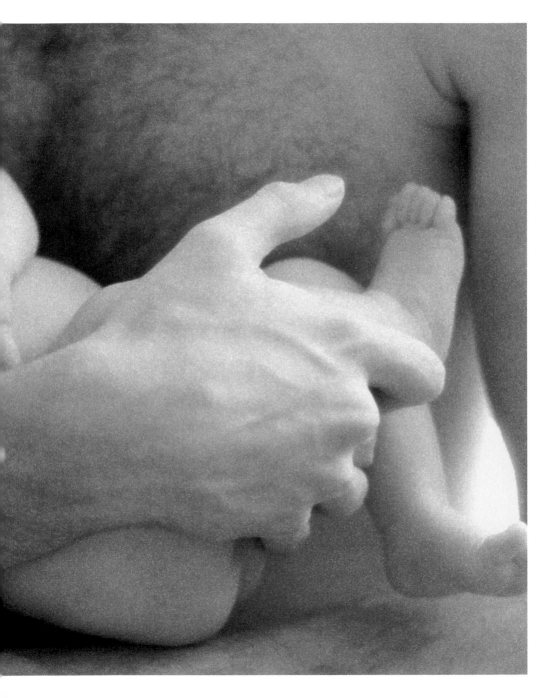

**THE STRONGER OUR BOND,
THE STRONGER I BECOME.**

YOU ARE MY ANCHOR.

A SECURE ATTACHMENT: THE KEY TO SUCCESS

Research now tells us that the single most important factor in shaping a child's future is the quality of the attachment to the parent. It has been confirmed that children who have secure attachments to their parents have more positive outcomes in a range of areas including personality development, learning, and the ability to form healthy relationships.

A seminal study demonstrated that babies who are held often and are securely attached to their parents in the first six months of life do not show elevated levels of cortisol, the stress hormone, in subsequent stressful situations. Stress is now known to be harmful to the development of brain cells. A nurturing relationship protects children from the impact of stress and helps them manage challenges throughout life.

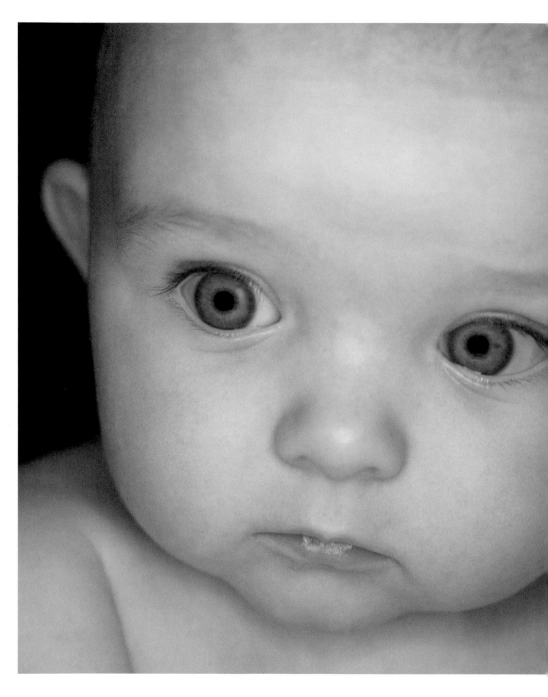

IT TAKES TIME FOR ME TO LEARN THAT
I WILL BE OKAY WITHOUT YOU.

I MAY BE SMALL, BUT I FEEL IT ALL.

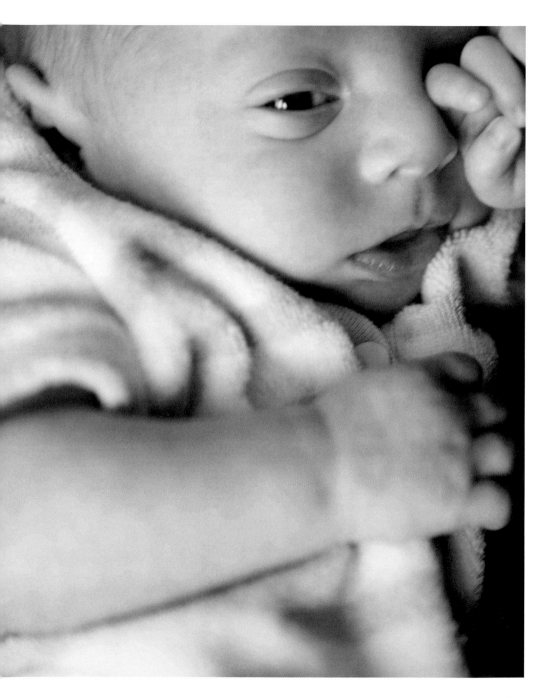

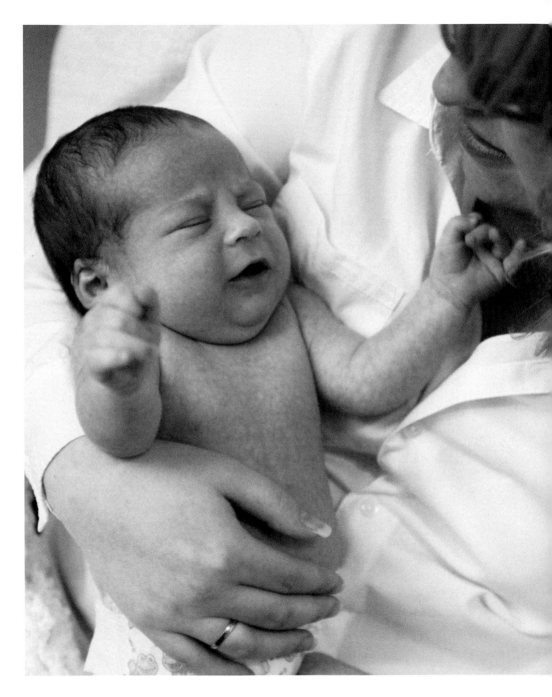

LOUD SOUNDS, BRIGHT LIGHT, OR JUST BEING UNDRESSED CAN OVERWHELM ME.

**WHEN I AM HUNGRY,
I COME UNDONE.**

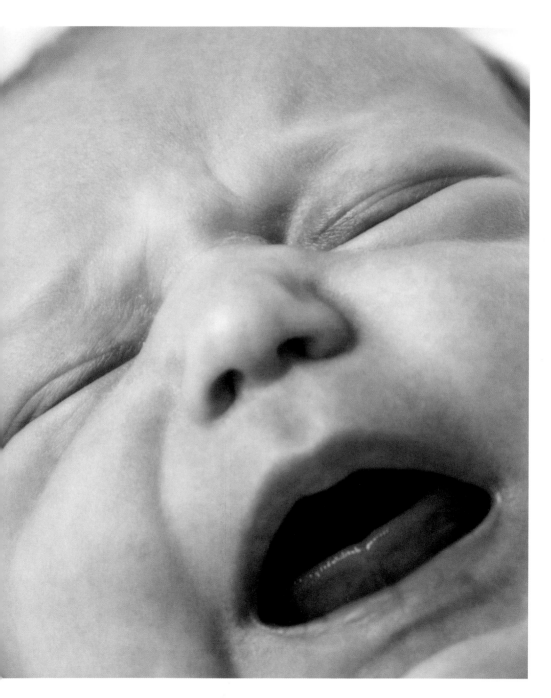

**WHEN YOU KISS MY BOO-BOOS,
YOU TEACH ME HOW TO BE KIND
TOWARD OTHERS.**

YOU ARE MY BUFFER.

YOU PROTECT ME FROM ALL THE NEWNESS.

WHEN I AM CRYING,
I HOPE YOU WILL COME.

I DON'T KNOW HOW
TO MAKE IT BETTER BY
MYSELF.

YOU CAN'T SPOIL ME

There has long been controversy about whether or not picking up a crying baby will spoil him or her. In a survey conducted by Zero to Three: The National Center, it was found that 47 percent of adults think that you will spoil infants under three months if you pick them up every time they cry. While this belief is prevalent in many cultures, it is in conflict with research findings that tell us the more we respond to babies' needs, the less needy they will become.

A groundbreaking study demonstrated that children whose cries are met consistently and promptly in the first quarter of the first year, cry less and sleep better in the rest of that year. The study also found that babies whose cries elicit responses tend to develop into independent, confident, and self-reliant children.

I KNOW WHAT I LIKE . . .

. . . AND WHAT I DON'T!

READ YOUR BABY

Research shows that reading and responding to a baby's cues are more important to brain development than any structured learning activity. Babies who feel understood learn more easily, have a positive sense of self, develop empathy, and can decipher social cues of others. As babies are seen, understood, and felt, they begin to experience and have a greater awareness of who they are.

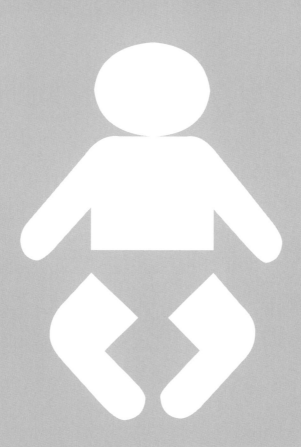

I LOVE BABY MASSAGE.
IT KEEPS ME CALM, HELPS
ME TO SLEEP, AND BRINGS
ME CLOSER TO YOU.

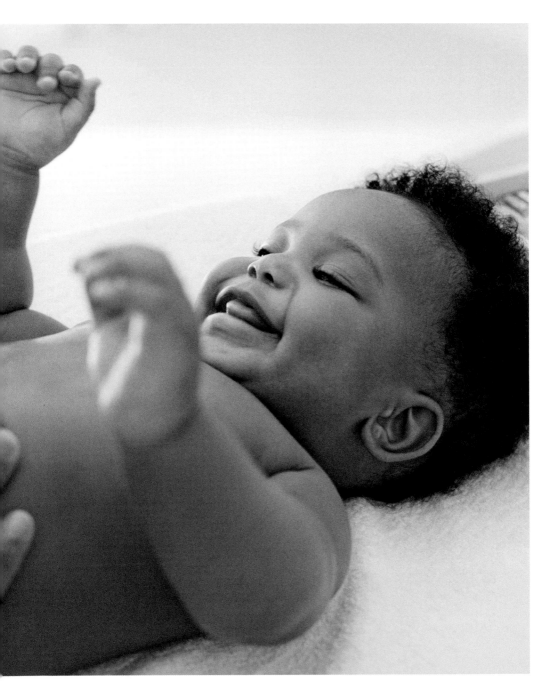

**TOO MUCH STRESS
CAN BE TOXIC TO MY BRAIN.**

**YOUR LOVE
MELTS MY FEAR.**

WHEN YOU LEAVE,
I WORRY THAT YOU WON'T
COME BACK.

I AM JUST LEARNING THAT
I WILL SEE YOU AGAIN.

I'M A MIMIC.

SHOW ME AND
I WILL FOLLOW!

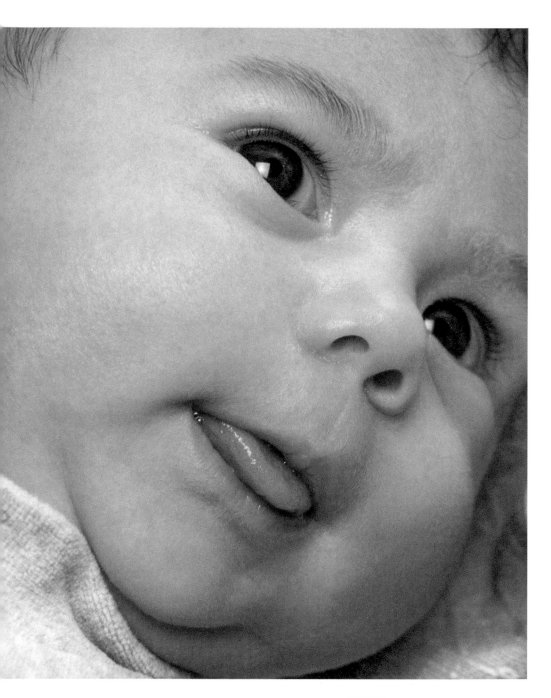

LOVING EXCHANGES LAST A LIFETIME

Loving interactions between parents and babies release oxytocin, commonly referred to as the "love hormone." Oxytocin reduces stress and increases trust. Recent research has demonstrated that the sufficient production of oxytocin in infancy is essential to the capacity to maintain healthy interpersonal relationships throughout life.

I LEARN FROM EVERYTHING I DO.

WHEN I SAY "OOOHH," AND YOU SAY "AAAHH," WE'RE TALKING.

WHEN WE "GET DOWN"
TOGETHER AND PLAY, I LEARN HOW
TO PLAY IN THE WORLD.

**WHEN YOU GET EXCITED ABOUT ME,
I GET EXCITED ABOUT LIFE.**

**YOUR LOVE
GIVES ME WINGS.**

**WHEN YOU FOLLOW MY LEAD,
YOU HELP ME TO BECOME A LEADER.**

LAYING A STRONG FOUNDATION

Comforting responses from adults help babies develop the capacity to soothe and calm themselves. This capacity is considered to be a cornerstone for emotional, social, and cognitive development, impacting such areas as concentration, attention, and the understanding of oneself and others.

THE POWER OF PLAY

The give and take of playing helps babies develop and learn about themselves, the world, and relationships. Babies learn best when adults allow them to be the leader and respond in ways that expand upon their play.

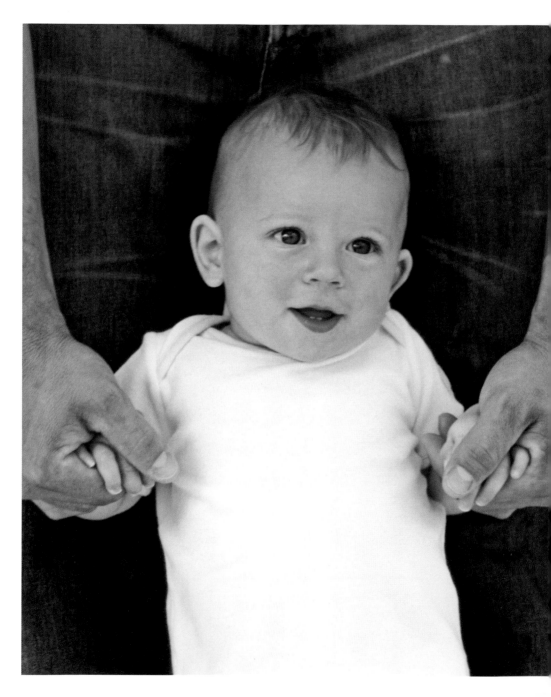

WITH YOU BEHIND ME, I FEEL SAFE ENOUGH TO TRY NEW THINGS.

**WHEN I CAN LEAN ON YOU,
I LEARN TO STAND ON MY OWN.**

**WHAT YOU GIVE TO ME,
I CAN GIVE TO OTHERS.**

**NOBODY KNOWS ME BETTER
THAN YOU.**

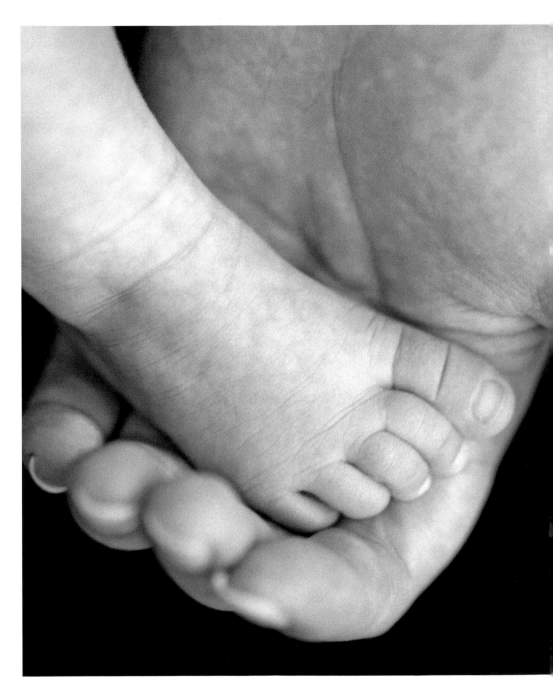

**YOUR LOVE PREPARES ME
FOR THE JOURNEY.**

RECOMMENDED RESOURCES

BOOKS

Barnet, M.D., Ann B. and Richard J. Barnet. *The Youngest Minds; Parenting and Genes in the Development of Intellect and Emotion*. New York: Simon & Schuster, 1998.

Bowlby, John. *A Secure Base: Parent-Child Attachment and Healthy Human Development*. London: Basic Books, 1988.

Elliot, Lise. *What's Going on in There? How the Brain and Mind Develop in the First Five Years of Life*. New York: Bantam, 1999.

Gerhardt, Sue. *Why Love Matters: How Affection Shapes a Baby's Brain*. New York: Brunner-Routledge, 2004.

Heller, Sharon. *The Vital Touch: How Intimate Contact With Your Baby Leads to Happier, Healthier Development*. New York: Henry Holt & Company, 1997.

Johnson & Johnson Pediatric Institute, *The Importance of Touch*. Cincinnati: Johnson & Johnson Pediatric Institute.

Johnson & Johnson Pediatric Institute and Zero to Three, *The Magic of Everyday Moments*. Zero to Three, 2000.

Karen Ph.D., Robert. *Becoming Attached: First Relationships and How They Shape*

Lief, Nina R. and Mary Ellen Fahs (ed). *The First Year of Life: A Guide to Parenting*. New York: Walker and Company, 1991.

McClure, Vimala. *Infant Massage: A Handbook for Loving Parents*. New York: Bantam, 2000.

Montagu, Ashley. *Touching: The Human Significance of Skin*. New York: Harper and Row, 1986.

Our Capacity to Love. New York: Warner Books, 1994.

Pruett, Kyle. *Fatherneed: Why Father Care is as Essential as Mother Care for Your Child*. New York: The Free Press, 2000.

Stern, Daniel N. *The Birth of a Mother: How the Motherhood Experience Changes You Forever*. New York: Basic Books, 1999.

Stern, Daniel N. *Diary of a Baby*. New York: Basic Books, 1990, 1998.

VIDEOS AND DVDs

Amazing Talents of the Newborn, Johnson & Johnson Pediatric Institute

Begin with Love, hosted by Oprah Winfrey, Civitas

Ten Things Every Child Needs for the Best Start in Life! T. Berry Brazelton

The Baby Human, Geniuses in Diapers

The First Years Last Forever, hosted by Rob Reiner, I Am Your Child Video Series

To Be A Father, hosted by Ray Romano, I Am Your Child Video Series

RECOMMENDED WEBSITES

Civitas (www.civitas.org)

International Institute of Infant Massage (www.infantmassageinstitute.com)

Parents' Action of Children (www.parentsaction.org)

Johnson & Johnson Pediatric Institute (www.jjpi.net)

Zero to Three: The National Center (www.zerotothree.org)

ACKNOWLEDGMENTS

THERE ARE SO MANY PEOPLE WHO HAVE INSPIRED THIS BOOK and helped to bring it into the world. I'd like to acknowledge the countless mothers I have worked with who, despite the lack of support in their lives or struggles in their own childhoods, came to my programs with open hearts and minds, wanting to give their children the love and understanding they may never have received. I'd like to thank Doris and Leon Hatkoff, who taught me about a parent's ability to focus on their children with a tenacious generosity and an infinite capacity for being available, supportive, and loving. And to the entire Hatkoff clan, especially my siblings, Susan and Craig, and their spouses and their spouses' families, who all share the ability to pour love, opportunities, and sweetness into their children, a tradition I revel in seeing passed down through the generations. A very special thank you to Juliana and Isabella, who have taught me about the power of love from the moment they were born. And my warmest welcome and thanks to Jack, Chloe, and Riley, whose beautiful spirits are steady reminders of how a parent's love helps a child grow.

My deepest thanks to Chris Culler, Tom Harriman, Dorothy Henderson, Sonia Orenstein, Gay French-Ottaviani, and Victoria Patricof for their input, edits, and expertise; the Institute for Infants, Children & Families of the Jewish Board of Family and Children's Services for their nurturing and extraordinary training; Wendy Sarasohn and Ellen Whyte, my personal *doulas*, who encouraged this production from the start; Marcia Patricof for her feedback and hospitality, both of which helped me reach the finish line; and Annie Abram whose brilliance and friendship continually fuel my creativity. And finally, many thanks to Carolyn French for her enthusiasm and commitment to delivering *You Are My World* and to Marisa Bulzone for being the midwife.

ABOUT THE AUTHOR

AMY HATKOFF is a parenting educator, writer, filmmaker, and advocate. She has been working with parents and children of diverse backgrounds for more than 20 years. In 1995, she was asked to translate the groundbreaking research on infant brain development into an accessible language for parents for Rob Reiner's widely acclaimed video *The First Years Last Forever*. She has brought that information to hundreds of parents, teachers, and caregivers through seminars and lectures in hospitals, corporations, doctor's offices, schools, welfare hotels, homeless shelters, and community organizations. She is co-producer of the award-winning documentary *Neglect Not The Children* and co-author of *How to Save the Children*. Ms. Hatkoff is a graduate of the Institute for Infants, Children & Families, the Parenting Education and Family Support program of Wheelock College, and Hamilton College.

Published in 2007
by Stewart, Tabori & Chang
An imprint of ABRAMS

Text copyright © 2006 by Amy Hatkoff
Photographs are courtesy of the following
collections: Jupiter Images: front cover,
back cover and pages 2, 5, 16, 21, 22-23,
37, 45, 51, 52, 56-57, 72, 76-77, 85, 86.
Getty Images: pages 8, 11, 12, 24, 26-27,
28, 31, 34, 42,48-49, 61, 62-63, 64-65, 68,
71, 75, 82, 87-88, 90. Fotosearch: pages
15, 38, 41, 58, 79

ISBN: 978-1-58479-591-9

Editor: Marisa Bulzone
Designer: LeAnna Weller Smith
Production Manager: Anet Sirna-Bruder

The text of this book was composed in
Avenir and Bickley Script.

Printed and bound in China
10 9 8 7 6 5

Stewart, Tabori & Chang books are available at special discounts when purchased
in quantity for premiums and promotions
as well as fundraising or educational use.
Special editions can also be created to
specification. For details, contact
specialsales@abramsbooks.com or the
address below.

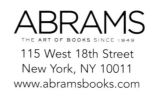

ABRAMS
THE ART OF BOOKS SINCE 1949
115 West 18th Street
New York, NY 10011
www.abramsbooks.com